SIMPLE STYLE

THE ELEGANT, UNCLUTTERED HOME

SIMPLE STYLE

THE ELEGANT, UNCLUTTERED HOME

LISA SKOLNIK ◆ RIMA A. SUQI

FRIEDMAN/FAIRFAX
PUBLISHERS

A FRIEDMAN/FAIRFAX BOOK

Please visit our website: www.metrobooks.com

© 2000, 1996 by Michael Friedman Publishing Group, Inc.

Library of Congress Cataloging-in-Publication Data available upon request.

ISBN 1-58663-017-2

Editor: Francine Hornberger
Art Director: Jeff Batzli
Photography Editor: Wendy Missan
Production Manager: Camille Lee

Cover design: Howard P. Johnson, Howard Communigrafix, Inc.
Front cover photograph: © Steve Gross and Susan Daley, design by Melissa Price
Back cover photograph: ©Dominique Vorillon, design by Christopher Coleman

Color separations by Colourscan Overseas Co Pte Ltd
Printed in China by Leefung-Asco Printers Ltd.

3 5 7 9 10 8 6 4 2

Distributed by Sterling Publishing Company, Inc.
387 Park Avenue South
New York, NY 10016
Distributed in Canada by Sterling Publishing
Canadian Manda Group
One Atlantic Avenue, Suite 105
Toronto, Ontario, Canada M6K 3E7
Distributed in Australia by
Capricorn Link (Australia) Pty Ltd.
P.O. Box 6651
Baulkham Hills, Business Centre, NSW 2153, Australia

To Dylan, whose generosity of spirit and intellect has sustained us in many ways. You have been an eternal source of reason, balance, and inspiration to us both.

Thank you to the staff at Michael Friedman Publishing Group, particularly to our editors, Francine Hornberger and Wendy Missan.

CONTENTS

INTRODUCTION

In this hectic age, probably the most meaningful gift we can give ourselves is a nurturing home, one that instills in us a sense of peace, pleases us aesthetically, and most importantly, meets all of our wants and needs. For, unlike the public spaces we frequent or our places of employment, our homes must accommodate a broad and ever-changing array of activities. Our homes must house our families; offer enough space for repasts, diversionary pastimes, and relaxing moments with friends; do double duty as offices, gyms, and recreation centers; and hold all our possessions.

Each of these functions has its own ground rules. Where families are concerned, the permutations can be staggering. Some of us live alone and can configure or outfit our homes exactly as we please, but others have children or aging parents to consider, all of whom bring their own sets of special considerations to the proverbial mixing bowl.

The way we use our homes is another matter. Some of us yearn for casual, open environments while others opt for formal arrangements with individual rooms. Those with large families or the desire to entertain often need spacious kitchens and dining areas to accommodate these activities. Still others need enough room to fit their offices into their living spaces, which may add equipment or an employee or two to the load their homes must hold.

And finally, all of us must have room to situate, show off, and/or store the items we use to support our lifestyles. In essence, we need our homes to house our possessions. Besides the prosaic furnishings and accouterments of everyday life, we may also have hoards of technologically advanced equipment for our endeavors, be these working at home or working out. And we may also have equally ample inventories of belongings for hobbies.

In other words, we have stuff—lots of it. Yet it's important that furniture and belongings don't get the upper hand when we're designing our homes. A living room bogged down with too many overstuffed chairs or knickknacks is cramped and uncomfortable. A family room invaded by gym or electronic equipment has little room left for its owners, which makes watching television or playing games next to impossible. And a dining table covered with the trappings of an activity is impossible to use for eating.

While these scenarios may seem fairly innocuous, they're actually critical issues that affect the quality of life for any homeowner who must live with them. In all of these situations, possessions have become impediments to a fulfilling daily life. Environments must be planned carefully and sensibly in order to meet the far-reaching and always-evolving requirements homeowners may have.

Mies van der Rohe was right when he said, "Less is more." Living with simplicity—organizing and scaling down possessions and eliminating clutter—can cure chaos, enhance environments, and streamline lives. And it can be achieved effectively, and with style, by any homeowner willing to put forth the effort to plan, pick, and stick to essentials.

But banish the assumption that living in this manner, and creating such an environment, calls for the spare, sleek residence epitomized by Mies and the Modernists. Decorating simply and effectively doesn't involve a specific style; it doesn't even require sticking to the confines of any particular decor. Almost every style can be adapted to the premise, whether it has a contemporary, traditional, romantic, country, ethnic, or eclectic tone.

Nor does it mean that the effect ultimately created in a home need be pristine, austere,

ABOVE: With appropriate planning, every style can be adapted to the tenets of simple design. Here just a few bold strokes, most notably an oversized armchair in a neutral tone and boldly striped informal textiles, were used to evoke country comfort despite the fact that no one element is specifically rustic in style.

minimalist, or bland. Rooms can and should be wonderfully designed and comfortable, but their function should determine the elements necessary to achieve this state. For instance, the furniture in a small space can be of the cushy sit-and-sink variety; there just shouldn't be so much of it that it overwhelms the room. Consider using fewer sofas that each offer up more seats per piece. You can deploy bold patterns and bright colors to adorn any part of your home, as long as they're carefully kept in check and don't compete with each other. Almost anything can work, if it's implemented appropriately.

Getting Started

While every space—and the circumstances that dictate its design—is unique, there are certain givens that apply to all situations. The most universal is the adage "Form follows function," coined by Louis Sullivan, although this doesn't imply that the design of a room should be strictly spartan and utilitarian.

Indeed, the way a space or room eventually looks is due to five important considerations:

- Who's using the space?
- What's going on in it?
- Where is the action taking place?
- When it is being used?
- Is it all working properly?

By asking these five questions before and during

ABOVE: No single element should be allowed to overwhelm a room. Here an elaborate bedstead is balanced with other elements that are far more streamlined. The window treatments are simple and modern, while the lines of a tapestry-covered chair are very spare.

the process of decorating a room, it's possible to plan and execute a space that works well. Hopefully, this will also lead to an environment that is supremely functional, impeccably well edited, and attractive all at the same time.

Planning
the Space

Start with "Who's using the space?" and "What's going on in it?" A room in which the entire family will lounge around and watch television will be markedly different in terms of furnishings, finishes, and layout than a living room reserved for special occasions. The same is true of a dining area used for daily meals as opposed to a more formal room, or a master suite compared to a children's bedroom. These first two questions set the stage for the framework of the space and relate to its very being. The type of pieces to choose to fill the space, the ways to address walls, ceilings, and floors, and the way the furnishings will be arranged all depend on the answers to these questions.

Next comes "Where is the action taking place?" This question will determine how to lay out the space. For instance, a fireplace would be the natural spot to anchor seating areas. But if the room also holds the television set, working out a way for the two elements to share the space successfully is essential, since both tend to be focal points and these two activities can be complementary or mutually exclusive, depending on the season. Solutions include turning the seating area on a diagonal to face both elements, or breaking the room up into smaller groupings.

Thus, determining the use or uses of each space, and resolving how different tasks can be accomplished in one area, is critical to the success of the environment.

"When is the space being used?" is also an important consideration. It may be used for one function during the day and another at night, such as a den that doubles as a children's playroom or incorporates a home office. If a room does double or triple duty, these functions must be incorporated into the room's design, and allowances must be made for all the activities to function smoothly. Toys or office paraphernalia should all have their own spaces, preferably in nooks and crannies that will keep them out of view. And lighting factors also impact this consideration. A room that receives bright sunlight, for instance, may need opaque blinds or the television set will be unviewable during the day. Weighing all these aspects of when a room will be used will help you to assess, plan, and refine the way the space will be laid out.

After these first four questions have been carefully considered, it's possible to create an environment in each room that will fulfill the needs of its occupants. However, this is when the decorative aspects come into play, and it's critical to be realistic and prudent about what goes into every space. Ask yourself what's really necessary to include in the room and be honest about whether it will really be used. Then plan furnishings to fulfill basic needs first. Use this as the take-off point for adding extra pieces, but be careful not to add anything that might be superfluous.

Since our lives are constantly in flux and the way we use a room can literally change overnight, every room begs for a reevaluation on a fairly routine basis to assess its effectiveness. We may decide to work, or merely work out, in our homes and have to adapt them accordingly, often requiring quick implementation. Nothing should be etched in stone; flexibility is critical to making a home meet the needs of its owners.

Implementing the Plan

Planning the function of each and every room in your home is just the beginning, for designing a home is an ongoing endeavor that takes careful consideration. And there are no hard and fast rules that dictate its progress.

Thus it's possible to commit to many facets of a design first—style, color palette, or specific furnishings—but ultimately the task of pulling together a cohesive and functional home unencumbered by needless extras lies in uniting these three components. So it's important to keep in mind the basics that go into creating a great decor, but equally important not to let them overwhelm the process.

STYLE

Style can be pure period, with options ranging from historical choices such as Neoclassical, Colonial, or Victorian, to contemporary selections such as Postmodern, High-tech, or New Age Shabby Chic. But keep in mind that the furnishings that evince some styles are far less comfortable and flexible than others, and pure adherence to any style limits the possibilities of what can be done in a room.

This concept may account for the advent of eclecticism, one of the most popular decorating options today, especially for a simple, functional home. Eclecticism allows us to pick and choose the best or most useful parts of various styles to apply to our home decor. A sensible way to decorate a home, eclecticism is much easier to execute in bits and pieces rather than all at once. But keep in mind that eclecticism isn't a license to throw everything together in one big and busy pot. It is still important to adhere to the basic principles of planning and design, which include creating a mix of furnishings and accessories that balances color, form, and scale.

ABOVE: Intricate architectural details go from ornate to elegant cloaked in one subtle hue. Equally subtle colors on the furnishings and the walls of the room help tie the room together.

COLOR PALETTE

Color is one of the most effective ways to give a room or a whole house new life. Spaces can go from cool to warm, cozy to expansive, or subtle to sumptuous, depending on the shades used to cloak them. Color can also be used to highlight a room's strengths (such as interesting architectural details) or mask its weaknesses (radiator covers or mismatched materials). And the power of color doesn't stop at mere cosmetics, for it can also affect our emotions and perceptions, thus influencing the way we feel about our environments.

Color is a tool that demands thoughtful consideration, especially if your goal is a simple home that isn't burdened with excessive design details.

ABOVE: Far from spare or sleek, this living room still manages to exude simplicity thanks to careful editing. Large elements from myriad periods are employed, unified by texture and hue.

So keep in mind the following pointers:

•Cool and pastel colors can make a room seem larger and reflect light; warm and bright colors have greater visual weight than cool hues; and warmer colors are easier to live with and more "forgiving" than cooler colors.

•Limit yourself to two or three hues in each room. Choose a dominant color first, then add accent colors.

•Complementary colors are as unlike each other as possible (they're strong hues in their strongest forms), so to create a subtle color scheme use milder variations of these colors (such as pink and mint instead of red and green).

•How color is perceived is relative to the lighting in a room, so check color choices under all lighting conditions. Paint plywood boards with the colors you want to use and check them over an entire day and night to see how light plays off the hue in every type of illumination.

•Colors reflect off each other, so schemes should be planned and tested out before they're implemented. In addition to checking the plywood samples for lighting effects, study how the colors work together.

SPECIFIC FURNISHINGS

Style and color are important, but the furnishings and accessories that you need, want, or choose to include in a room ultimately have the most impact on the way the space feels. While keeping everything to a minimum can limit the potential uses of a space, too much stuff undeniably leads to a cramped, cluttered environment. So it's important to strike a balance in each room that maximizes its functional aspects.

In effect, balance guides the process that establishes the layout of a room. It begins with the largest or most noticeable furnishings, such as a soaring armoire, a voluptuous grand piano, a plump oversized sofa, or a sweeping table.

ABOVE: Balance starts with the largest or most noticeable elements of a room, such as this bulky armoire. Baskets and pots on top elongate and refine its proportions without actually adding clutter. A single chair breaks the perfect symmetry of the scene, adding interest and actually instilling the sort of balance achieved by offsetting a large focal point (namely the armoire).

Other objects can come into play as well: a massive piece of art (such as a sculpture or wall-sized painting) or equipment (such as a large-screen television or pieces of fitness equipment) garners just as much attention as the furniture. These pieces can be used as building blocks to arrange and array the rest of the room.

Once the focal point is determined, the rest of the room can fall into place. In a very large space a layout can be symmetrical, asymmetrical, or multifocal (several focal points can be accommodated), but it is important always to keep in mind the principle of cause and effect. Every object causes a reaction in a room (a grand piano, for instance, must be balanced with equally grand seating), and addressing that reaction is crucial to creating the proper sense of balance.

On the following pages are a series of well-designed and effective environments that are attractive, comfortable, livable, and most important, supremely functional, thanks to their simplicity. No matter what the decorating style, function came first in planning and decorating these attractive and successful environments. The process involved setting limits on furnishings and accessories, and displaying, housing, and storing possessions in an organized and practical fashion. The results are homes that are well planned, clutter-free, and beautifully designed.

FIRST IMPRESSIONS

INSIDE AND OUT

First impressions are important, yet the areas of our residences that we and our guests encounter first don't always receive their just due. We often give little thought to the elements we use to adorn the façades, entryways, or foyers of our homes.

Consider the exterior of an abode. It's obviously the first thing anyone about to enter the residence notices, but it's usually an afterthought in the decorating process. A dilapidated or worn wooden door surrounded by weathered brick goes from shabby to smart when it's washed with a strong but simple coat of bright paint. The same holds true for a balcony or porch, which can be transformed from nondescript or unsightly to extraordinary and inviting if treated in the right way. A large jardiniere or a few simple boxes filled with flowers will add style, while sturdy benches or chairs turn these sweeps into serviceable spaces. And in the areas just inside the front door, a few functional furnishings can be used to reclaim dead space.

Usually, however, when there is money to be spent on projects for the home, "hard-core" interior objectives such as new kitchen equipment or living room furniture tend to take priority. And the amount of money and thought required to repaint the exterior of a home, refurbish a porch, or even outfit a foyer with closets and cabinets can often seem staggering, and might make the project seem not worth undertaking.

Yet the outsides of our residences and the spaces that serve as conduits to the inside are as important as interior spaces, since they form a prelude of what's to come. An unkempt, dilapidated, or unattractive exterior is not inviting for neighbors and guests. And an entryway or foyer, however architecturally promising that is misused—that is, totally empty, too full, or merely unsuitably arrayed—is unwelcoming and wasteful.

Porches, decks, patios, and outdoor rooms are also spaces that should be carefully considered, for they can become positive additions to a lifestyle if shrewdly composed. Some can be put to good use by providing extra square footage for a small residence; others can make a routine residence unique by adding architectural cachet or taking advantage of beautiful or interesting surroundings outside a home.

PAGE 16: The simple façade of a Georgian home gets a touch of grandeur from a handsome, whitewashed portico.
PAGE 17: Coating a traditional element, such as this door, with an untraditional hue makes it far more engaging, especially since it is surrounded by a conventional period pediment in a neutral shade.
OPPOSITE: Porches, patios, decks, and other behind-the-home spaces deserve as much attention in planning your home's design as so-called first impression spaces. This carefully planned porch is a wonderful spot for outdoor entertaining, and because its design is so architecturally elegant, it requires only a couple of potted plants and a chaise longue for embellishment.

Maximizing First Impression Spaces

Ultimately, it pays to give all these spaces the same respect, attention, and effort given to individual rooms. This means making them as simple, functional, and aesthetically powerful as possible. Approach the task of decorating them as you would a space with more specific purposes, imposing the same kinds of restraints on the process to make sure they're not excessive or ineffective. Although making the most of these spaces is an objective, part of that goal includes making sure they aren't overwhelmed with such extraneous features as inappropriate or fussy decorative embellishments or too many trappings. First impression spaces must function as efficiently as the other areas of your home, and must exhibit the same sort of style. This chapter will help you to make the most of these all-important spaces. Following are some basics about each type of space to keep in mind.

OPPOSITE: Consider porches, decks, patios, and outdoor rooms as extensions of a home that also have to be carefully composed. Here a simple table and chairs are all that's necessary amid the bounty of a beautifully landscaped environment. A simple wood trellis also comes in handy to define the space and mask a brick wall. ABOVE: A trio of strong hues turned this unassuming entryway into a powerful portal without adding any extraneous elements.

Exterior Façades

The view from the street says a lot about who inhabits a place, especially if it's a shabby one. A rundown or ragged appearance will rub off a bit on the interior, regardless of how carefully decked out it may be. Plus, if a house is the only one on a street that looks bad, this could affect both the relationships the owner has with the neighbors and the resale value of the place.

Simple good grooming can go a long way toward improving or lifting the exterior of a home.

Paint is the most obvious resource to employ. A plain but perfect coat of color, whether subtle or strong, can add lots of cachet to virtually any structure. When details such as doors, casements, or pediments are punctuated with just one contrasting color, that cachet increases exponentially. And there are many other options that are equally easy. Awnings can add dignity, an interesting door can give a place character, and flowers in containers can be quaint.

Other improvements require a bit more thought or money, but yield enormous returns. A patch of land becomes an alluring front yard when reclaimed with a fence or a garden plan. A decaying fence can be replaced with something solid, well built, and attractive. Architectural details can be layered on a plain façade to make it look more significant.

But ultimately the wants of an individual must be carefully balanced against the constraints of the structure and the limitations determined by its location. An elegant Victorian painted in catchy

TOP: Color proved to be the perfect element to use on this entryway; it added both depth and definition to its rudimentary design. BOTTOM: Simple plank shutters flank both windows and doors on this home, adding a nice architectural touch. OPPOSITE: This contemporary residence is striking to begin with, but it becomes stunning with the addition of color. A golden yellow softens the structure's sharp lines, while a bold rust highlights its architecture. Both hues relate to, and complement, the other materials employed in the building, such as flagstone and wood.

colors can look excessive or overblown, and may seem unsightly instead of appealing. A row house laden with ornamentation can look garish if its adjoining companions are decorated in a simple and elegant manner. Take into account the architectural period of a residence and the nature of its surroundings before making any changes.

Foyers and Entryways

Stepping straight from the street or an exterior hallway into a residence can be psychologically jarring. Every home should have a transition area that allows you to shake off the outside as you adapt to the new environment and get your bearings inside. Ideally this transition occurs in an entry or foyer (though some homes lack this luxury), which should be attractive and welcoming, yet at the same time ordered and efficient. Consequently it is best not to clog these spaces with clutter, but rather to compose them with carefully chosen furnishings and accessories that fit the scale of the space and enhance its practicality and appearance at the same time.

A small table, topped with a wall-hung mirror, and a chair are great pieces to begin with; they add instant organization to the space and increase its functionality. The table can hold mail or a bowl for keys; the mirror visually enlarges a space and

ABOVE: Architectural details, such as classic shutters and a portico supported by stylized pillars and encrusted with vines, have been layered on this plain façade to make it look more significant. OPPOSITE: A small table and chair are great pieces for starters in an entryway; they add instant organization to a space and increase its practicality. If there are no specific architectural boundaries to the space they are even more practical, since they also give definition to the expanse by breaking it down into an intimate little area.

allows occupants and guests to check their appearance as they go out or come in; and the chair provides a spot to sit and wait for a moment or to put on shoes and boots. Consider also a bench or a loveseat, a hat and coat rack, an umbrella stand, or a small chest for scarves, hats, and gloves. Keep scale in mind: oversized pieces will be unwieldy in small foyers, while delicate pieces will be lost in grand ones.

In actuality, an amply sized entryway can often serve several purposes for those enterprising and clever enough to utilize it properly. It can be equipped with a series of built-in cabinets or even outfitted with the trappings of an entire home office. Or one large freestanding piece—such as an antique trunk or chest that can also serve as bench-style seating—can provide storage and add warmth and intimacy to the space.

In homes that lack a specific entryway or foyer, try improvising. Just a bit of stolen space

TOP: Even a tiny entryway can serve several purposes. A row of hooks and a Windsor settee add function to this space, while a subtle harlequin pattern on the floor imbues it with elegance. BOTTOM: A narrow banquette topped with a cushion and pillows turns the space below this stairway into a seating niche. OPPOSITE, TOP: A dramatic staircase speaks for itself in a foyer; it's best to keep everything else to a minimum. OPPOSITE, BOTTOM: A fairly conventional foyer becomes both airy and grand with several cleverly employed design tactics. Trompe l'oeil topiaries that flank the door save space; a leggy metal bench is almost weightless yet functional; and a chubby chest that offers up storage is tucked out of the way, yet still shows, under the stairs.

can be used to work wonders. A folding screen or a shelving system carve a few square feet out of a living area adjacent to the doorway. Fill the space with only one or two pieces but make them exquisite or daring. The result will be a space that is stunning and serviceable at the same time, and it will create a memorable first impression for your guests.

Hallways and Stairways

Hallways and stairways can be much more than mere passages to other areas of a home. Like an entryway or foyer, these spaces can often be put to good use. Even more to the point, the tiny bits of space these areas afford can actually be polished to perfection, making them the show-pieces of an abode.

Start by taking stock of the space, then enhance it accordingly. An ordinary stairway can become stately and grand with a beautiful banister and a rich Oriental runner, or interesting and intimate with a deeply hued background and art on the walls. Narrow hallways or landings can become more spacious with a slim console table topped by a wall-hung mirror, while space with more depth can accommodate a trunk or chest that offers up added storage. The space available in a hall is often the perfect spot to showcase collections; arrange

artwork or artifacts on walls in a composition that covers a whole wall for effect.

Whether the decor is subtle or bold, simplicity is crucial in spaces of this nature to keep users from feeling too hemmed in. Keep the actual pieces that impinge on the floor space to a minimum, and balance the look carefully. Austere surroundings can be spiced up with an ornate mirror or console, while streamlined pieces can work in a space that has an elaborate wall treatment or complex paint job.

Porches, Decks, and Patios

Whether it's possible to use your porch, deck, or patio all year round or just two to three seasons of the year, these spaces can become functional, multiuse rooms if they are furnished with enough skill to allow them to be used to their fullest capacities. Consequently, it is important to design them just as carefully and attractively as any room inside the home. Editing the pieces used to decorate these spaces is equally

OPPOSITE: Just a few simple pieces are all that is necessary to add warmth and utility to an austere entryway. Keeping them simple and all in the same vein emphasizes the architectural identity of the space. TOP: A Southwestern feel is created in this foyer with a few well-chosen accessories. BOTTOM: With the additional of a table and benches, a balcony adjoining a home office is even more serviceable. It does double duty as a work space and dining area.

THIS PAGE and OPPOSITE: It doesn't take much to turn a balcony, patio, or porch into an outdoor room that increases the square footage of a residence and offers the best views in the house. Essentially, just tables and chairs were used to transform the spaces above and opposite into dining and lounging areas. These pieces are effective because their styles are selected so as to allow the surroundings to speak for themselves.

important, since the scenery outside them should be the main attraction.

Some porches are fully enclosed and therefore enjoy many of the same amenities as a regular room, such as heating or air conditioning, full windows, and decent (even luxurious) flooring. These spaces usually boast the best view in the house, since they often overlook the garden. Consequently, it is important to be strategic when it comes to furnishings, since there may be little if any wall space against which to place sofas or other large pieces.

Decks and patios boast no such amenities, and the constraints that apply to a porch—no walls to anchor furnishings—are magnified in these spaces. So pick pieces that can work together and be gathered into cozy groupings that will anchor themselves. Three or four large chairs, for example, can be arranged around a low table, facing each other or opening out to take advantage of the view.

When decorating outdoor or semienclosed spaces, it is also important to consider weatherproof furniture that can withstand temperature extremes and the elements. Indoor furniture will probably be fine on a protected porch, but the pieces used on patios and decks have to be hardy if they're intended for year-round use or will stay out even during winter months. Opt for

mildew-resistant fabrics and fillings, and extra coats of varnish or paint on the pieces used in these spaces. For open areas, massive wood pieces made of weather-resistant wood that will weather as time goes by are ideal; accessorizing them with soft waterproof cushions is one way to make them more comfortable.

Arranging these spaces can be tricky. Even though they lack formal entrances, they have definite traffic patterns, so it is necessary to plan the layout as meticulously as an indoor room. But ultimately it is most important to pay homage to the most prominent aspects of these spaces: what lies beyond the actual boundaries of the "room." Nothing can really compete with the beauty of nature, and the whole point of the space is to enjoy the great outdoors. The furnishings can be modest or simple as long as the space stands out.

Outdoor Rooms

There are all sorts of ways to take advantage of a rolling lawn or lush garden. It is extremely easy to integrate structures or areas into these expanses that can be used for eating, entertain-

OPPOSITE: A corner of a patio is turned into a restful oasis with two simple wicker chairs and some pots of flowers. ABOVE: An arbor is creatively devised with translucent cream drapes instead of foliage, and furnished with a simple dining set veiled in a matching cloth. Despite the simplicity of these materials, their height and lavish use transform the space into a charming, yet formal dining area.

ing, or merely relaxing. Gazebos, tiny cabinlike structures, detached pavilions with or without some sort of shelter from the elements, or ad hoc rooms carved alfresco style out of a portion of the yard, can all be set up simply and stylishly on a seasonal basis.

Follow the guidelines suggested for other spaces in this chapter, but augment them with a healthy dose of creativity. For instance, pick the most exotic spot in a garden for an outdoor room, then furnish it accordingly. A cluster of chaise longues, chairs around a table, or even a bench made comfortable with cushions, can anchor a whole activity area. Again, simple weatherproof furnishings are the key, arrayed to let the scenery steal all the attention.

LIVING SPACES

The phrase "living room" can be a bit misleading. Unlike rooms where the usage defines the space—such as the kitchen, the bedroom, or the bathroom—"living" involves so many different activities that they could never take place all in one room.

In times past, homes had several rooms that have since melded to form the modern-day living room. Today the closest we get to these rooms is reading about them in Henry James novels, or viewing them in historic mansions such as those in Newport, Rhode Island. These rooms—with names like morning room, parlor, or drawing room—basically corresponded to where one spent different hours of the day, as opposed to referring to the activities in which one actually took part in these particular rooms.

Historically, the morning room was the place where one—usually the lady of the house—would spend her or his morning. This wasn't necessarily the spot to have breakfast, but rather to spend quiet time, reading or writing. The morning room was also used to receive guests who might drop by; the parlor, too, was used for this purpose, as well as a place to while away the afternoon. The drawing room was reserved for more formal evening entertaining, as well as a place to congregate after dinner for drinks and conversation. Since the purposes of these rooms

PAGE 34: The star of the living room is often the fireplace; here it provides a natural centerpiece around which to arrange a couple of comfortable Arts and Crafts–style chairs and a leather ottoman. It also serves as a platform on which to display a favorite painting or photograph, or a collection of first-edition books. PAGE 35: Every room has "moments," an area of grouped items that creates its own little style story. Here, a period lamp rests on a stack of books next to a lacquered tray that holds three globes, all on top of an antique chest set against a brilliant red wall. ABOVE: Creating a simple interior is of course much easier when there is a lot of space to work with. This open-plan space features a lofted office area, a well-hidden kitchen and subtle dining area, and living area all in one. High ceilings, white walls, and a neutral floor provide a perfect backdrop to showcase classic furniture pieces by Eileen Gray, Frank Gehry, and Marcel Breuer.

ABOVE: A floor plan that provides for an easy flow of foot traffic around specifically designated areas for socializing and eating is always a good call. It's apparent that most of the time spent in this room is at the table in the background, which is situated just adjacent to the kitchen, within close enough range to have a good conversation with the family chef. Two chairs and a small table are grouped for quieter conversation or reading. Other furniture pieces are placed on the periphery, thereby keeping the traffic flow uninterrupted.

were pretty clear-cut, their design and decoration were also relatively straightforward, illustrating a "form follows function" philosophy.

In America, the Industrial Age brought an economic boom, and with that an increase in building, which soon translated into an increase in the size of homes. The keeping room—which traditionally was the room in the home in which all activity, from cooking and eating to gathering and sleeping, occurred—began to disappear, as separate kitchen, living, and dining rooms were incorporated into the design of homes.

And so design dilemmas ensued. What is this room meant for? How does one furnish a space with such cross-over functions? As with many other rooms these days, the living room often finds itself doing double duty as family room, home office, workout room, or part of a "great room," ironically very similar to the concept of a keeping room.

Defining Your Living Space

In such a space, keeping things simple can be a challenge. But if rationally thought out, even this multipurpose room can be functional and stylish, while properly pared down. The first step is to

OPPOSITE: A house with striking furniture and an amazing view of a well-manicured lawn, great pool, and interesting sculpture doesn't need much else. Besides the view, what holds this room together is consistency of flooring (industrial gray carpeting), of wall material (glass), and of furniture (classic pieces, upholstered in black leather). ABOVE: A cozy coffee table and pair of wicker chairs are casually grouped close enough to the kitchen to almost effortlessly refill a cup, but far enough away to ensure that there's enough room to move around the counter. A smooth, poured concrete floor unifies both areas, and is warmed by the wood in the kitchen and the complementary wall colors of rich, golden yellow and aqua.

choose a style consistent with the way you really live. If your idea of a living room is impeccably matched formal seating in a set arrangement, but you don't ever entertain in such a way, you run the risk of having a room that looks completely staged, or worse, a furniture showroom. Chances are that neither you nor your guests will feel comfortable here, which completely defeats the room's purpose. Style should not be forced; it should develop through

the years as you acquire new tastes, and therefore objects, and rid yourself of others that no longer seem appropriate.

Terence Conran, a true style maker and promoter of good design, wrote in *The Essential House Book* (Conran Octopus Limited, 1994): "There is no reason why you shouldn't indulge a certain style of decorating. But if you can discern which elements of the style appeal to you, and adapt those to your own way of life, you are more likely to be successful than if you try to fit the style into an environment for which it was never intended."

Once you have an idea of the style of the room, consider what you want from the room in terms of function, when and how often you expect to use it, what mood you wish to convey. Is it a dark, more romantic space, or a lighter and brighter one? Will you spend hours reading by the fire or watching TV with the kids, or will you just occasionally retreat to the living room after entertaining dinner guests? All of these questions must be taken into consideration before you begin arranging the furniture. Remember that, with good planning, the living room can become the most versatile room in the home.

Start with a centerpiece, something that will be the "star" of the space. In a bedroom this is usually the bed. In a living or family room there

OPPOSITE, TOP: Does it come as any surprise that a legendary hair stylist, whose claim to fame is a perfectly simple, angled bob, would live in a perfectly simple, mostly glass home with perfectly simple, angled furniture? Of course not. In this arrangement, the color yellow serves as a unifying element: on the sofa, picked up again in the small bowl on the table, and also in the choice of flowers. OPPOSITE, BOTTOM: Cozy doesn't have to mean cluttered. A cushy couch, with down-filled pillows, floats seductively in front of a wall of picture windows (there is enough room behind it to adjust the window treatment). Springtime tints on the throw pillows and curtains add a touch of color, while maintaining an overall soft look. ABOVE: The star of this room is actually in another room. It's the staircase, and its dramatic ascent is accented by the relative lack of furnishings in the entryway. In the foreground, an unusual grouping of four armchairs around a table means the space could be used for meals or business meetings. Wood, in different but complementary shades, unifies the space, as it is used on almost everything—the walls, floor, staircase, door, and fireplace.

are a few options, and none of them should be too obvious. Try a fireplace, a grand piano, an entertainment center or armoire, a wonderful rug, or perhaps just an incredible view through a picture window.

Once you've selected the star, everything else can be arranged in relation to it. Keep things simple with pieces that combine beauty with brains— great to look at and super-functional.

A standout sofa with classic lines is an obvious choice, as is a selection of chairs, which can range from the cushy and comfortable to the more sleek and sophisticated. It's important to choose fabrics that are as durable as they are stylish. Interestingly enough, many contract fabrics—traditionally used for office or institutional furniture—have become much more fashion-forward, and are now being used for domestic interiors. These fabrics may cost more, and you'll have to buy them through an architect or interior designer, but they are made to specific code for high-use environments, and therefore often last longer than other fabrics.

A coffee table adds a lot of function—a place to stack sumptuous style books, stash the selection of remote controls, do homework, or just put up your feet. That said, an oversized ottoman is often a wonderful substitute for a coffee table. Many manufacturers now make them in an

OPPOSITE: This layout is slightly cluttered, but not overwhelmingly so. Its design remains fairly successful because thought was given to traffic flow, and furniture situated to accommodate that flow. Again, the star of this room is the fireplace, and a pair of sofas are situated at right angles to take in that view. There is plenty of room to move around the coffee table, as well as behind the sofas, to additional seating.
ABOVE: Unify with color—or the absence of it. White is classic and a little high-maintenance, but the effect is undeniably elegant. Here, the walls and textural fireplace surround all wear white, as do the glass vases on the glass table, subtly placed sconces, table lamp, and the area rug.

incredible range of styles, with legs or without. Our personal favorite is the storage ottoman, an upholstered piece whose top comes off to reveal a space large enough to hide magazines, books, or even a few throw blankets.

Arranging the pieces you've chosen is quite another matter. Obviously you need a plan that provides for an easy flow of foot (or paw) traffic, as well as one that promotes socializing. It's important to remember that the way you place the furniture will dictate the traffic pattern, so try to find an arrangement that directs traffic around areas of activity. For example, if you float a sofa in front of an entertainment center, most foot traffic will fall behind the sofa, not in front.

If you have a large space and expect to entertain large groups of people, the best plan calls for spreading smaller seating areas throughout the space in intimate groupings. However, a smaller space means making do with less, in terms of both square footage and furniture. Arrange pieces in ways that will promote conversation. A sofa or chair should have some small table or other surface nearby to place drinks or a small plate of hors d'oeuvres. End tables, like coffee tables, can be double-duty pieces, serving to display favorite decorative accessories or perhaps just one elegant lamp.

ABOVE: For those who are worried that their style looks too simple—perhaps too many solid colors or too much wood—introducing some pattern is often an effective way to add some life to a room, without overpowering it. Here, curtains were created using blocks of color sewn together; the blocks pick up on existing colors in the space and add others that work together. OPPOSITE: Groupings of furniture are key to socializing, and while there are plenty of pieces in this room, there is a certain symmetry to their arrangement. Note the pair of leather club chairs, placed not as expected (flanking the fireplace), but still adjacent. The armchair, foreground, has its mate lurking in the background.

Storage Solutions

Many living rooms, regardless of size, are also used as family rooms, so the decor and arrangement must be flexible enough to accommodate these diverse uses, and storage becomes critical in achieving this goal. Think cabinetry. Often used to achieve a more contemporary look, custom cabinetry is designed and fitted for a specific space. Not everyone has the budget necessary for such made-to-order luxury, but luckily there are a host of other options.

Built-in storage, such as window seats that lift up, provides the perfect place to hide magazines, books, and even toys. Built-in shelving, around a fireplace, doorway, or window, simultaneously serves to make an architectural statement and to display items like books or an array of china, glass, or just about any other collectibles. Keep in mind that stylistically it's better to group objects (especially in odd numbers) than simply to scatter them around a room. Beyond being a stylist's

OPPOSITE: You can bet there's a TV, VCR, and possibly a few other components hidden inside this armoire, a favorite storage piece. A chair and table are arranged for easy viewing, and are located next to the kitchen, meaning that a snack is never more than a few steps away. ABOVE: Traditionally, armoires were used to store clothing and accessories, and were placed in a bedroom. Today, they are made in every style and size imaginable so that no matter what your interior design, there's an armoire to fit your taste and your budget. It's a worthwhile investment—a substantial piece of furniture that looks good and can store just about anything. The one shown here probably serves as a linen closet.

"trick of the trade," this approach also creates a more simplified, streamlined space.

One of the most popular and cost-effective options is without a doubt the armoire. Traditionally armoires were used in the bedroom to store clothing and accessories. Today's armoires come in virtually every size imaginable, and are used for everything from their original intended purpose, to general storage for linens or china, to an elegant entertainment center, the most common family

room usage. Doors open to reveal space for a TV, VCR, cable box, and stereo, plus specially designed drawers or shelves for video and cassette tapes, compact disks, and of course, all the corresponding remote controls. Doors close and all the clutter is hidden.

Creating Unity with Color

So far we've addressed the selection and arrangement of furniture, and storage options for living and family rooms. However, it's become more and more popular to combine living, dining, and kitchen areas into one "great room." A common problem with such a space is creating a sense of unity—the feeling that while three or more different activities occur in this large room, it is really just one cohesive space. The answer: color.

The simplest place to create unity with color is right under your feet. That's right, the floor. The exact nature of the material doesn't matter; whether wood, ceramic tile, vinyl, or even wall-to-wall carpet, using the same flooring throughout a space is a subtle but exceedingly effective way to ensure that it feels cohesive. For those instances in which you want to use a different type of flooring (carpeting doesn't work well in kitchens, for example), be sure the color remains consistent between the different materials.

OPPOSITE, TOP: This space demonstrates a clever, even subtle, use of color repetition. Look closely: the colors of the walls—blue, hot pink, and red—can be found in the upholstery fabric of the chairs. With all that color on the walls and chairs, it was probably a wise choice to keep the area rug in a more subtle coloration, and paint the ceiling a shade of off-white. OPPOSITE, BOTTOM: Symmetry of objects is a surefire way to create a look that says simple, even though there may be quite a few pieces of furniture in the room. Here, a pair of chairs flanks the fireplace. On the mantel are a pair of potted plants; on the wall above it are a pair of sconces. Even the mirror shows great symmetry, featuring a pair of cherubs. ABOVE: Bound by blue and white, this serene sitting area features stripes of baby blue on its walls and throw pillows; this same color blue is picked up in the pattern of the armchair cushions and on some decorative objects.

ABOVE: Some say black is the absence of color. Whatever it is, it's one of the most useful hues in both fashion and interior design. Suitable for framing, black puts everything in perspective, whether a print, a fireplace, a speaker cover, or an iron table. It's a way to break up a stark white room for the color-phobic. OPPOSITE: Besides color, another way to bring the elements of a room into sync is with texture. In this light-filled space, wicker chairs and side tables and even the sisal area rug work together to create a design scheme that blends well with both wood and iron pieces.

Walls are another area just begging for color. The choices here, however, can be more difficult. Before taking the plunge, tape color swatches to your wall and note how their qualities change throughout the day with the change in the room's natural light. Or, if you have the patience (not to mention budget), buy a quart of each color you are considering and actually paint a patch of your wall, or paint the sample colors on plywood boards. This will help to ensure that you remain happy with your choice after the entire room is painted. (See the "Color Palette" section in the introduction for more specifics on choosing the right colors.)

Finally, try to repeat colors throughout the kitchen, living, and dining areas. If your kitchen cabinets are stained green, for example, perhaps the same shade of green is also found in the upholstery of the dining room chairs or the pillows on the living room sofa.

Before you know it, you will have transformed this important room into a truly streamlined, stylish space that's as functional as it is fun to live in, day in and day out.

KITCHENS AND
DINING AREAS

Once upon a time, the kitchen was one of the most straightforward rooms in any home. It had one—and only one—purpose, namely the preparation of meals. Historically the kitchen was by no means a glamorous place, and was whenever possible situated in a building separate from the main house to assure that food preparation and food consumption remained two very separate activities. Even when the kitchen finally made its way to the main house, it was sometimes relegated to the basement, housed underground so as to contain the smells and sounds associated with food preparation.

Today, the sights, sounds, and smells of cooking are considered so comforting that we welcome them in our homes. Cooking and eating can take place at the same time—today, a house may have a large eat-in kitchen rather than a separate kitchen and dining room. Furthermore, the demographics of the people preparing the food have changed drastically. The days of full kitchen and serving staffs are for the most part long gone. As women move out of the home and into the workplace, the responsibility for preparing food is increasingly being transferred to other family members. Too, with families' busy schedules, preparation time, as much as dinner itself, is a chance for everyone to be together.

PAGE 52: Log cabin life can indeed be luxurious, as shown in this kitchen. Cabinets are stained a dark shade of green, which helps to enhance the fact that almost everything in this room is wood, and fronted with divided glass, providing an intimate view of the contents. The hood (mandatory for professional stoves) is cleverly encased in its own cabinet, thereby ensuring a streamlined look. PAGE 53: It's all in the details. Walls wear cool shades of blue and green, sparsely adorned with a colorful stencil, a flea-market-find chair is freshened up with white paint and a classic damask cushion, and a basic wood table showcases vintage linen and a sculptural candelabra. ABOVE: Some rooms speak of a simpler life with a nod to the past. This kitchen features a vintage refrigerator, a can opener mounted on a window, retro lighting, and an island counter that is reminiscent of a folding card table. Another giveaway—this kitchen is devoid of a dishwasher, at least of the machine-age variety.

ABOVE: Simple is a snap when storage is as abundant as in this large kitchen, with its walls of chrome-colored cabinetry, warmed up by well-placed blocks of richly stained wood, and ample natural light streaming in through a facing wall of windows. Four anchored stools, upholstered in cobalt-blue leather, serve the dual purposes of adding a touch of color and inviting guests to socialize and snack at the center island.

The commercials featuring do-it-all moms who rush home from work to whip up a great meal are misleading. It's probably more realistic to find any combination of Mom, Dad, nanny, and even kids running in and out of the kitchen, grabbing a bite as they can. In today's society, the dinner ritual can be tough to preserve.

For this reason, the housewares market is now flooded with appliances and gadgets designed to make every step of food preparation faster, easier, and often convenient to the point of requiring virtually no thought at all. Name almost any formerly labor-intensive food preparation process, and chances are that there's now a machine to do it. Witness the overnight sensation that bread machines caused several years ago. Everyone wanted to wake up to the smells of freshly baked bread wafting through the house. It was the bridal shower gift of the year. But where are many of those machines now?

In fact, all those fancy appliances that purport to make our lives easier may ironically be making life a little more complicated. After all, these glamorous gadgets each take up a certain amount of counter space, and how many things can you really fit on a counter before it starts looking like the housewares section of a major department store? Beyond that, you have to figure out how to actually use these high-tech items,

OPPOSITE: When storage space is sparse, shelving works twice as hard, providing storage and showcasing colorful ceramic pieces that are taken down and used as needed. Mismatched chairs around a farmhouse table, old-fashioned beadboard used as wainscoting, and a big basket of freshly picked tomatoes send the clear message that this room was meant for relaxing. ABOVE: The combination of white walls and wood can be simple to a fault. But what's a pattern-phobe to do? The answer is twofold: a splash of subtle color to distinguish the doorway, and a classic black-and-white vinyl checkerboard floor, as shown here.

since so many involve understanding how to pro-gram the timers, settings, and the like.

Perhaps we should heed Henry David's Thoreau's advice: "Our life is frittered away by detail. . . . Simplify, simplify." This can be done in several ways. The most obvious is to get rid of any small countertop appliances or gadgets not actu-ally used more than, say, the first week they were purchased. Think of this as clearing your closet of all those oh-so-trendy clothes you bought on a whim, wore only once, and then donated to a local thrift store. When was the last time you used that bread machine, or juicer, or bagel cutter? The answers to these questions quite possibly coincide with some pretty embarrassing hairstyles that you'd rather forget.

For those who can't stand the thought of cleaning house so ruthlessly, there is a compromise situation: put it all away. That's why creative cabinetry, attics, basements, garages, parents' homes, and rental storage spaces exist. Absence may make your heart grow fonder for these pieces, but chances are that once they're out of sight, they're truly out of mind—not to mention out of your usage vocabulary.

Planning an Efficient Kitchen

So you've cleared out the stuff, and now what? Time to evaluate the efficiency of the room you have, or for those starting from scratch, the room you'd ideally like to have.

Obviously, space planning and storage are the key elements in a well-designed kitchen. Think

OPPOSITE: Long, seamless stretches of one material (as in the countertop of solid surfacing material) help unify a room and draw the eye to a focal point, in this case a picture of a dramatic sunset. A small butcher-block table serves as an extra surface or workstation when necessary. ABOVE: A very restrained space, characterized by rectangular and square planes, is livened up a bit by cobalt-blue tiles behind the range; this same color is picked up in the terrazzo countertop, and by a strategically placed glass bowl. Two bar sinks take the place of a more traditional kitchen sink—a dishwasher must be hidden somewhere underneath.

about the activities that take place in this room. Once the cook's solitary domain, the kitchen has now become the center of domestic life, encompassing one or more eating areas, food preparation spaces, and perhaps space for lounging or even a corner for a small home office.

A properly thought-out, well-designed space will simplify everyday life by making food preparation faster and more efficient, providing storage for items you already own as well as those you will acquire in the years to come, and creating easily navigated traffic patterns in this most popular room in the house.

Since the 1950s, kitchen designers have used the "work triangle" configuration as a starting point. The triangle refers to the placement of the three areas most often used in the kitchen: the stove, the refrigerator, and the sink. The theory is actually very mathematical, based on the concept that there are "ideal" distances for placing these areas. If you draw a line from the sink to the refrigerator and then to the stove, the length of that line should be no more than twenty feet. Obviously this leaves a lot of leeway in playing with the lengths, but the general rule is that the spatial relationship between sink and stove is most important, since these two areas are used most often during food preparation.

ABOVE: Sometimes the emphasis in the term "simple style" is put on the latter word. Here, batches of bold color, grouped together, complement each other and bring cheer to the room. A cobalt-blue hutch plays host to a collection of pottery; those same colors are repeated in the tablecloth and dinnerware.
OPPOSITE: A counter of calm dominates and exudes a zen-like vibe, with its rich wood complemented by soothing green cabinetry. Storage space is plentiful, thereby keeping the clutter police at bay, and socializing is restricted to standing room only at this waist-high counter sans seating. However, the open plan with adjacent dining area means the family chef needn't be completely secluded.

Storage Solutions

Once you've figured out the basic configuration of the space, it's time to think about storage options, starting with cabinetry. This is an equally important process to examine

thoroughly, for several reasons. First, cabinetry can be extremely expensive and mistakes cannot always be corrected cheaply or easily. Second, cabinetry is the primary form of storage in a kitchen, and the options are innumerable.

Cabinets can be custom designed to store just about anything, from the usual dishes and pots and pans to spices, stepladders, even kitchen sponges. Any item, no matter how small, can command its own special space, so it's best to try not to get too carried away with compartmentalizing. After all, the goal here is to simplify.

One immensely popular and practical cabinetry option is the kitchen island. Whether stationary or moveable (some people put them on wheels), the island is an excellent place to put a sink or a range, or just to use as an extra work surface, since it is easily accessible from several sides. Islands also provide added storage for many things: dry foods (like colorful beans or pastas in glass-fronted drawers), pots and pans stored underneath, knives either in drawers or in vertical holders built into the countertop, or collections of heirloom china, silver, or other memorabilia.

Furthermore, islands become a natural focal point for entertaining while preparing a meal for friends. Everyone knows that all the true dinner party action really occurs in the kitchen, and what better place is there to gather around,

OPPOSITE: Built-in cabinetry was once a standard feature in many homes. The kind shown here was normally found in hotels or inns, and for good reason—a slew of storage space for the requisite fine china, silver, stemware, and linens. ABOVE: A curved wall of woven sisal adds texture to an otherwise seamless space that appears to be at the same time retro and modern. Note that the hutch, with its law-office credenza looks, is gussied up with outrageous hardware.

sitting on bar stools and sipping wine, while helping a meal come together, or just watching.

Arranging the Dining Area

Most of us eat at least three times a day. While this is obviously necessary for basic nourishment, eating is also a very social activity. More and more, families and friends gather to celebrate

holidays, anniversaries, or other events around a meal. Considering the importance eating has in our lives, it's not surprising that many areas in homes have evolved to accommodate this activity. Dining is no longer confined to the formal dining room; we now have more informal areas as well, including breakfast nooks, kitchen counters, banquettes, and even screened-in breakfast rooms, as well as outdoor dining areas.

The dining room as we know it didn't really appear until the seventeenth century, and only in middle-class houses at that. Stationary tables, meant only for dining, appeared on the scene, and naturally it wasn't long before all the accouterments needed to dress those tables became part of the standard decor.

This new room required appropriate chairs, place settings of china and silver, various styles of glassware and different types of linens, and, of

TOP: A room with a view like this doesn't need much more. The Adirondack rocker brings the feeling of patio living indoors. An indrustrial-style pendant light presides over a somewhat formal table, which is relaxed by the company of a quartet of country chairs, complete with gingham cushions. BOTTOM: A sliver of space can hold much more than expected if the pieces are as simple as possible. Witness this alcove, stuffed with a huge dining set. The spare lines of the massive table are softened, but not made fussy, by a "set" of mismatched chairs. A row of metal candlesticks adds a country touch without detracting from the clean, uncluttered feeling. OPPOSITE: Less can be more inviting: note the long bench seat for sitting or sprawling, old plank floors, beadboard wainscot, and divided-light windows that wear nothing more than a wonderful view. Mismatched chairs tell visitors that relaxation is the norm here.

course, suitable furnishings in which to store them, like sideboards, buffets, and breakfronts. By the mid-nineteenth century the dining room was laden with every type of accessory imaginable. Today there is cutlery and accompanying china for every conceivable course, to the point where a place setting of china or silver can include a dozen different pieces for foods ranging from fish and shellfish to meat and even ice cream. And the more stuff we have, the more clutter we're prone to have.

The idea of paring down and simplifying that may have worked so well in the kitchen is not so effortlessly applied in the dining room, however, since items used in dining areas tend to have more sentimental associations than, say, a set of cookware. The good stuff—china, silver, and crystal—is traditionally acquired in one of two ways, either as wedding gifts that a couple painstakingly chooses and registers for at the start of a life together, or as heirloom pieces. Thus these items carry much more meaning than a set of napkins purchased for a summer feast, and consequently are not the types of things that would be thrown away. So, what can be done?

The two most obvious options are either to store these treasures or to spotlight them as a collection. Fortuantely, there are many big, beautiful storage pieces perfect for dining areas

OPPOSITE: Well-placed curves dominate this large space: in the ceiling, the chandelier, chairs, wall, and even the custom carpet. These curves keep this dining room, with a table set for twelve, from looking like a conference room. Kept fairly simple, the space is unified by the splashes of color— cobalt blue accented by black, even in the well-chosen artwork. ABOVE: Simple is easier when there is a lot of space. This interior features barn-style beams and low partitions instead of walls, creating a feeling of openness. The owners wisely chose not to push the furnishings, picking classic pieces to showcase (like the Cab chairs around a custommade table) against a perfectly smooth pickled wood floor.

of any style and budget. These large breakfronts, sideboards, and china cabinets can make a singular style statement on their own, or just meld into the existing decor. Better yet, they'll accommodate all those place settings, plus linens and a lot more.

Spotlighting these treasured pieces serves several purposes as well. They will be out of the way, but they'll also look more like art objects. For example, a friend showcases the Blue Willow plates she inherited by hanging them on a bright red wall in her dining room. Another friend stacks antique linens in her dining room in a breakfront with glass doors, creating an invitingly beautiful sea of white and off-white. Other places you may choose to feature such pieces include the tops of armoires or cabinets, shelves or picture rails, and fireplace mantels.

TOP: Bright red walls set the stage for this vibrant, yet airy space. Other primary colors are brought out in the multicolored chairs, increasing the room's vitality. An area rug placed atop a bare wood floor defines the dining area. Little other embellishment is needed. BOTTOM: Simple style defined. Although this is a kitchen and dining area, it has none of the traditional trappings of clutter usually associated with these spaces. A vase of bright flowers is just about the only decoration included. OPPOSITE: Simple style is sometimes reflected in symmetry—here a symmetrical and indeed, formal design keeps a very full wall from looking overly flamboyant. The circle theme is repeated in the prints, the frames, even the chair backs and window treatments. Again, the curvaceous theme means that a simple feeling exudes from a space with clutter potential.

BED AND BATH

Every home needs a sanctuary, a place to escape from the hustle and bustle of every-day life, to retreat, re-energize, and relax. Increasingly this harmonious space tends to be either the bedroom, bathroom, or some combination of the two in a suite-type arrangement. Regardless of the precise configuration, it's almost impossible to rid oneself of mental baggage in a room that's physically cluttered or impractically designed. It's essential to create a space that's clean-lined and serene.

However, as important as that may be, some say that the bedroom has traditionally been the "stepchild" room in a home—the room that gets the least attention, the last room to be renovated (if renovated at all), the room where the least money is spent on both decoration and upkeep. Yet, over a third of our lives is spent sleeping, presumably in a bedroom, and most of us have more than one such room in our homes.

PAGE 70: We spend a third of our lives reclining on this piece of furniture, the bed. Whatever the style, the setting should radiate serenity. Here, a whitewashed bedstead wears linens in inviting shades of blue and white, with an amazing backdrop, courtesy of Mother Nature. PAGE 71: Sleek and seemingly simple, this sink set-up is not for everyone. But those who do take the plunge will revel in its elegant faucet, affixed to the wall, not the sink itself (a very contemporary nod to a very old concept), and the deep bowl of frosted glass with a green tint. TOP: This small twin bed is known as a daybed. Fabulously functional, it's a sofa and bed all in one, and comes in very handy in small spaces. Some styles are available with a trundle accessory, an extra mattress hidden underneath that can be pulled out to make the twin bed a double.

OPPOSITE, BOTTOM: A small attic room with exposed beams, A-frame walls, and a strategically placed antique iron bed is inviting. True to period style, the bed wears a matelassé coverlet, with a an extra-warm comforter for cooler nights "stored" at its foot.
ABOVE: Simply beautiful—a semicircular window with a wonderful view is also simple in its symmetry, which is echoed in the pairs of nightstands, lamps, and fluffy pillows. A quilt adds a touch of the old-fashioned to an otherwise contemporary space.

ABOVE: The four-poster bed is a classic, elegant design that's adaptable to almost any interior style. This one is especially deluxe, with an upholstered headboard and fabric panels (that echo the yellow wall stripes) that can be drawn to completely hide the bed from view. Again, symmetry comes into play with matching console side tables and floor lamps.

Arranging the Bedroom

Lately the bedroom has been evolving to encompass much more than just the requisite bed and nightstand. Indeed, as with so many other areas of a home, the bedroom is becoming a more multipurpose space, and as such can be a more complicated space that increasingly lends itself to more clutter.

Placing the Bed

Let's start with the basics. The centerpiece of every bedroom is, of course, the bed, and the positioning of it is a crucial consideration. Many design magazines advocate "floating" the bed in the middle of the room. While this does create a dramatic visual effect, and is a wonderful way to showcase a truly stunning piece of furniture, it's important to consider the size of the room before making this sometimes impractical move. For

TOP: Use of color need not always clutter an environment. A well-chosen accent piece, such as an armchair upholstered in a rich red fabric, picks up on the red in the framed map above the bed, and the bedding as well. Placing the chair in a corner helps maintain an easy flow of traffic. BOTTOM: Maximize guest room space by opting for two twin beds, rather than one large double or even queen size bed. Here, a very simple theme is carried out by means of color and symmetry. Two twin beds dressed as twins: matching sheets in a classic ticking-like pattern, traditional plaid pillow cases, warm woolen blankets. Above the beds hang two similarly sized and framed prints, while below lie two small sisal rugs.

75

ABOVE: In this case, the concept of simple and spare may have been taken to an extreme that would make architect John Pawson proud. A bed and only a bed, in a dramatically angular room that's painted a bluish shade of white. Nothing more, nothing less. With bones like this, who needs furniture? In reality, storage remains out of sight to maintain the architectural integrity and power of the room. The variety of angles reflects light, which thus creates an engaging sort of decorative treatment in and of itself.

those with very large spaces, and perhaps walk-in closets, we say, "Go for it," although it is worth mentioning that followers of the Chinese practice of feng shui believe that floating a bed is a mistake—for just as the bed floats in a space, the person who sleeps in it may find himself or herself going through life feeling a bit unanchored.

For those with smaller spaces, consider the following. Think about what other pieces of furniture need to be placed within those boundaries. If closet space is at a minimum, and other pieces like an armoire or dresser must pick up the storage slack, then floating a bed may not be the best idea. However, even in some small spaces the floating technique can serve to create unusually shaped areas or even alcoves that, if properly accessorized, become very utilitarian in their own right. Try creating small subspaces for dressing, reading, writing—the options are only limited by your imagination.

Sometimes it's best to just give in and place the bed in an offset alcove, or position the headboard against a wall. It may seem like a cop-out solution at first, but especially for those who want to make the most out of a smaller space, it can be an optimal situation. Often, especially in more contemporary spaces, designers will create a storage area around the headboard (much like the built-in cabinetry of a kitchen), which can be camouflaged to look like part of the surrounding wall. This not only makes that area visually more interesting, but provides a place to put clothing and accessories, books, and even the three sets of linens allegedly needed for each bed in the house (one on the bed, one in the laundry, and one fresh set waiting to be used).

For those in studio apartments, the ultimate solution for both sleeping and storage is a Murphy bed, a bed that folds up into a cabinet that, when closed, looks like a closet, armoire, or wall of cabinets. Often custom made, Murphy beds are by no means inexpensive, but prices will vary depending on complexity of design, materials used, and geographic location (in New York City, for example, where apartments are notoriously small, there's a bustling market for these beds). Some are very basic, with just a mattress, others incorporate shelves, drawers, or both in which to store bed linens, and some even feature overhead lighting to read by.

Accommodating Other Bedroom Furnishings

A bedroom is more than just a place to sleep, and as the functions of this room multiply, so do the types of often bulky pieces necessary to accommodate those functions. Desks or writing

ABOVE: One can never go wrong with shades of off-white, beige, and taupe, as shown here. This handsome and soothing bedroom is not devoid of furniture, it's actually rather full. But the design is successful due to the calm palette that's perhaps more inviting than intriguing. A bench at the foot of the bed can serve as a footrest for the chair in the foreground, a place to rest a bed tray, or as extra seating.

tables, big comfy chairs, stands for television and stereo components, computers and home office accessories, even various pieces of gym equipment, all need a place. Ideally that place would be in another room, but life in the 1990s dictates that

most rooms do double duty, and the bedroom is unfortunately no exception.

And so the ongoing conflict remains: how to retain the identity of the space while getting the most out of it. The answer, as always: simplify. Find ways to keep all extraneous, distracting, nonrelaxing matter out of sight and therefore out of mind.

In the case of home office equipment, the hottest trend is the "office in a box." When closed, this looks like an armoire or a small cabinet. When opened, it's a small but fully functioning office with a desk and space for a computer, fax, phone, lamp, memo boards, and so on.

Television and stereo equipment is easily hidden as well. Many homes are now wired for speakers in every room, so the actual control center can be located elsewhere and the music will still be heard in the bedroom. However, if a

TOP: Making every corner count, a chair (found at a flea market) is put to a new use propping open a door, thereby letting the breezes of summer filter in, while simultaneously holding court with an antique towel rack, used as a side table. An old apothecary lamp was rewired to be used as a sconce, and given a coat of white paint. BOTTOM: Everything old is new again—and looks it. These antique pieces are relegated to an attic space, where the bed is placed a few inches away from the wall so that it fits, and is dressed with a fabulously fresh chenille bedspread—just like at grandma's house. A small table and old lamp are the only necessary accessories. OPPOSITE: A room can fulfill more than one function while maintaining a simple, clutter-free style. The bed here could have been floated, creating more drama. However, space was saved by putting it against a wall, allowing room for a writing desk and an extra chair, which make this room more of a sanctuary than a showcase.

ABOVE: What was once a screened-in porch was converted into a bedroom, with the bed resting against windows. This can work, but be mindful that there may be a draft, which can be annoying, especially in cooler weather. Window treatments are very simple horizontal blinds, and the little exposed wall space is painted a soothing shade of blue-gray. Furniture is at a minimum: a side table, lamp for reading, and rocking chair. OPPOSITE, TOP: The designer here went for paradox: a super-simple, almost Shaker-style bed for a room that's very "decorated." Again, the symmetry of bedside furniture and lamps helps keep the overall style fairly orderly, as does the lack of other major pieces of furniture. OPPOSITE, BOTTOM: This vibrantly painted kid's room features a built-in unit for storing everything from books and toys on the top shelves to clothing in the drawers below.

home is not so high-tech and the main system is, say, in the family room, there are plenty of portable audio systems on the market with great sound. These small wonders are easily hidden but often stylish enough to be visible, their size makes them perfect for bedroom (or bathroom) use, and they won't wipe you out financially.

Gym equipment is another story. Whereas the 1980s witnessed the trend toward a large fitness station that worked every muscle group, the 1990s finds many of these pieces either at garage sales or functioning as very expensive coat hangers. Those who absolutely can't do without this equipment must work around it, perhaps placing it in an alcove that can be screened off from the rest of the room. Those with more minimal equipment—hand weights, mats, and a few videotapes—will find it easy to stow in existing drawers, armoires, closets, or even under the bed.

Coping with Kids' Rooms

Interestingly enough, beds that include storage or space-saving options in their design tend to be found in children's rooms. For example, captain's beds have drawers built into the base to hide clothing, toys, games, or—much to parents' chagrin—homework. Trundle beds, which have

an extra mattress that slides out from underneath, are perfect for sleepovers or unexpected guests. Bunk beds are perhaps the ultimate space saver, since two beds take up the same floor-space normally needed for one, and drawers can be built under the bottom bunk.

But even with all these space-saving and storage options, the hope of keeping things simple in a kid's room is perhaps unrealistic. This is, after all, the ultimate multipurpose space, used for activities as varied as sleeping, playing, and studying. As quickly as the room is picked up, it is messed up. Help can be found in a plethora of fun, colorful storage units, in a multitude of materials and price ranges. Shelving, big plastic boxes that stack, trunks and under-bed drawers on wheels all make life in this room a little simpler, if only for a few moments at a time.

Closet Ideas

Of course, the ideal solution for all these storage dilemmas is to have lots of closet space. In urban areas, such space is often but a dream; many apartment dwellers are forced to cram as much as possible into one or two closets, and must either come up with several creative storage solutions for a multitude of leftover stuff, or rent an off-site storage space to hold items they just can't part with.

OPPOSITE: Despite all the furnishings, possessions are actually kept to a minimum in this kid's room, increasing the likelihood that it will stay neat and organized. ABOVE: The contents of this closet can be hidden from sight behind a curtain that matches the walls perfectly. Shallow wooden drawers are an attractive and efficent way to store shoes, and a plastic bowl is a fun and practical way to store underclothes neatly.

Those with the inclination and the budget will find it worthwhile to hire a "closet consultant" who will come to your home, assess the storage situation, and suggest ways to reconfigure and reorganize closets to make optimal use of existing space. The consultant's suggestions are often implemented with a system of wire racks that, although by no means glamorous, provide amazing results. If hiring a professional is not in your budget, stores dedicated to storage carry all the organizational racks, boxes, hanging shelves, and other paraphernalia necessary to do it yourself, as well as a knowledgeable staff to help you choose the right items.

Walk-in closets can truly open the way to a simpler life. They can range in size, in style, and in price, but they're found in so many new homes these days that they're obviously here to stay, and for good reason. What's not to like about handsome floor-to-ceiling cabinetry for storing sweaters in summer or sundresses in winter? Taking its cue from the kitchen, this cabinetry

TOP: A child's closet can be kept neat and tidy if it is planned correctly. This well-organized closet features plenty of cubbyholes for storing everything from shoes to linens to a small gumball machine. A rod was also included in the configuration for hanging dress clothes. BOTTOM: A walk-in closet this size is any homeowner's dream—it is so large that it even includes room to accommodate a couch for contemplating the day's attire. Open and closed storage holds everything from belts and undergarments to sweaters and shoes.

is often custom designed, so a specific drawer or nook or shelf can be created for any particular item. In addition, walk-in closets are often designed to be large enough to function as dressing rooms, with full-length mirrors and perhaps even a chair or bench.

Organizing the Bathroom

This brings us to the one room, besides the kitchen, that has generally grown more in square footage than any other. The bathroom is getting bigger, which is indicative of the room's changing function from strictly utilitarian to a room that is also dedicated to relaxation. Whereas some may see the bathroom as a purely functional space where they rush to shower, dress, and run out the door, more and more people see the bathroom as a place to relax and unwind and

TOP: Mosaic mania at its finest! The use of different colored mosaic tiles usually works best when limited to one or two colors. However, if you must go all out, keep the rest of the room simple. As shown here, the tile is definitely the star, all other fixtures—from tub to toilet—just blend in.

BOTTOM: Today's bathrooms feature more furniture than in the past. This room nods to an earlier era with a footed tub and old fashioned fixtures, a wooden towel rack, framed prints, and a touch of stained glass in the windows. The color violet plays a major part in coordinating this room and updating it to look more modern.

take the time to light fragrant candles, bathe in scented waters, and decompress at the end of a long, hard day.

The recent boom in the once relatively obscure aromatherapy market means that bathroom products that were once fairly economical purchases requiring little thought are now more complicated. Consider soap, for example. The choice used to be fairly simple: deodorant, moisturizing, plain, or, in a few cases, scented. Now the selection is almost overwhelming. There's a soap to fit any color scheme, scent preference, shape, and style. There are even soaps with words carved into glycerin and others with a rubber ducky inside. But it doesn't stop there. Bath salts and scrubs, shower gels, and accessories like loofah mitts and invigorating back brushes were all once exotic items but are now selling like crazy and finding their way into bathrooms across the country. The trend is so strong that there's even a trade show devoted exclusively to aromatherapy and related products.

Fortunately, many such items feature packaging beautiful enough to be worthy of display. But add these to the other bath accessories that everyone from Calvin Klein to Liz Claiborne is designing these days—like a little cup for cotton swabs, a glass bowl for cotton balls, or a marble tissue box cover—and clutter becomes inevitable.

OPPOSITE: Here is a simple sanctuary in shades of white, located on an upper floor and therefore requiring no window treatments for privacy. A deep tub, retro-looking faucet with shower attachment, towels hanging from Shaker-style pegs, and a simple, yet elegant sconce all exemplify the ultimate in simple style. ABOVE: The spareness of this space signals true luxury—and a big closet somewhere nearby! A sunken tub, with a faucet that simulates a waterfall, is illuminated by natural light filtering through a glass block wall and bouncing off a large, strategically placed mirror.

Solutions today go way beyond the basic medicine cabinet, although this is still a good place to start. Medicine cabinets are getting bigger and better-looking, with adjustable shelving to accommodate the storage of objects galore.

Other options can be adapted to under-the-sink cabinet space (except in the case of the now-popular pedestal sink).

Increasingly, bathroom storage means shelving, whether strictly utilitarian or more decorative. Almost every nook and cranny can be utilized. Glass shelves have become a de rigueur high-style solution. Such shelving—in either clear or green glass with a beautifully beveled edge, suspended by high-tech wires—is very elegant and perfect for setting off beautiful accessories, but it is a bit high-maintenance.

Triangular-shaped corner cabinets are ideal for holding towels, linens, or cleaning supplies. Several catalogs feature shelving racks built to fit around and above a toilet. Even the space above a door or window can hold a discreetly placed shelf for storing stacks of fluffy towels.

TOP: Some prefer formal bathrooms—with custom window treatments that coordinate with upholstery, intricate molding, and antique furniture. The hutch here serves as a place to store towels and other bath-related accessories. The stone floor is a nice, subtle choice that blends with the decor, rather than competing with it. BOTTOM: For some, a free-form space is optimal, with as few walls as necessary. This configuration allows the non-timid to share the space, with one person soaking in the tub while another showers nearby. Again, nature provides a beautiful backdrop. OPPOSITE: Getting back to nature sometimes means literally bringing the outdoors in. Here, a stone wall adds a textural element to a super-sleek room that utilizes very modern materials with a slightly industrial edge.

WORKING SPACES

Thanks to new technology, our daily patterns of work and play are shifting. Though statistics say we devote more hours to our jobs than ever before, we aren't necessarily putting in those hours at the office. At the same time, our leisure-time activities, such as working out, writing, reading, studying, or pursuing a hobby, have also become a more prominent part of our lives, and are more diverse than ever before.

Yet all of these endeavors have one thing in common: they are increasingly being performed at home. In fact, the pool of activities we take part in at home is growing faster than the square footage available in our residences to devote to our pursuits. Thus "a room of one's own"—which early-twentieth-century British author Virginia Woolf posited as a prerequisite for writing—is an enticing ideal, but few of us have the luxury of possessing such an exclusive space.

In fact, it is the rare residence that has a surfeit of space; this is one resource there never seems to be enough of. While some may be able to devote a whole room to hobbies or a home office, most will have to make do with limited resources. Hence the rise of the multipurpose space for work or play, which can be a corner carved out of a larger area, or an entire room devoted to two or more activities. In many cases this space is shared, since several members of a household are often initiating their own pursuits at home these days.

If we plan carefully, some of us can devote a whole room to special pursuits and others can find a bit of space to mine for these needs. Sometimes a corner of a room is truly underutilized and can be easily altered to accommodate an office, gym, or hobby center. But in many cases it is necessary to steal a spot, pilfering whatever square footage we can from other areas of our homes. Making the most of these "mined" or "stolen" spaces, which are often compact or even minute, takes creativity combined with good planning and design.

Ultimately all these working spaces, whether large or small, allocated or mined, need to be functional and simply composed regardless of the style of decor. Furnishings can run the gamut from contemporary to traditional, casual to formal; the point is that they must be carefully chosen to serve several purposes and to fulfill the needs of each individual using the space.

PAGE 90 : New technology can fit right in with traditional furnishings. Here, the computer looks at home thanks to the straightforward look of the room's furnishings. It has also been placed right next to a window, which provides a simple and elegant backdrop as well as natural light. PAGE 91 : A large secretary can be as functional as a full-sized office, since it can house everything that's needed to get to work. OPPOSITE : Few of us have a whole room to devote to a home office or work space. It's often necessary to steal a spot, outfitting whatever square footage is available with compact, yet attractive, pieces.

Working in an overaccessorized home office, gym, or workroom can be counterproductive, since extraneous objects or inappropriate furnishings eat up available space and make it difficult to accomplish anything.

Following is a rundown of some of the specific types of work spaces you can create in your home, and some advice on how to keep them simple, appealing, and—most important— effective and efficient.

Home Offices

Millions of Americans are going home to work either full or part time, and for good reason. It means a thirty-second commute, no dress code whatsoever, and complete avoidance of office politics. But better yet, it means a tailor-made milieu that changes the very nature of the process. Working environments can be comfortable and relaxed rather than cramped or unpleasant.

While such technology as the personal computer, printer, copier, fax machine, and modem has made this all possible, it has also raised design issues: how do we keep all this equipment at home without it becoming overwhelming? These machines, coupled with the growing trend to work out of a home office, have in fact fueled a whole new market in the furniture industry, one

OPPOSITE: Dead space comes alive with the right accouterments. Here an alcove under a stairway becomes a practical work space with decorative, sensibly proportioned pieces that fill the space without overwhelming it. Accessories are also carefully culled and balanced to give the effect of an elegant tableau. ABOVE: With the right equipment, a working environment can be tucked away in the corner of any room. Here a desk and wall-hung set of cabinets serve as an entire home office, occupying just a corner of a den.

that emphasizes innovative pieces to hold an ever-changing array of equipment and an always-growing variety of needs. Thanks to such innovations, it is possible to eliminate excessive or duplicated furnishings and create environments that are streamlined and simple.

A single piece of furniture can become a complete office, as can a corner of any room. Since the equipment we now need is incredibly compact, the options are endless. Closets, bookcases, and kitchen cabinets are all contenders to become work spaces, and can be just as vital as a whole spare room. Thus any kind of room can be mined for a home office, from a formal dining room to a great room that has to fulfill many functions. But family rooms, dens, and bedrooms seem to be the biggest "recruits" for this purpose, since they usually harbor the most excess space.

Regardless of its location, creating the right kind of home office poses very specific problems. What about the file cabinets that won't fit where

TOP: Every unused nook and cranny has the potential to hold the bare necessities for a home office. This tiny alcove, filled with natural light and graced with an outlet, is a perfect case in point. A desk and chair turn it into a fully functional working space. BOTTOM: Since a home office doesn't have to duplicate a corporate setting, it can be an extension of the decor that already exists in a home. Here, pieces that blend utility with a high style quotient are used to carve a home office out of one end of a room. OPPOSITE: For those with enough space, it's possible to create a sleek set-up that can serve multiple functions. The round end of this desk can also be used for conducting meetings.

they need to go, the desk not designed for a computer, or the shelves that are so laden with supplies and equipment that they're out of control? Anyone can pack all sorts of sophisticated accouterments into a space, but making that space effective, as well as comfortable and attractive, is truly a challenge.

Just as a home office should not be an attempt to duplicate a corporate setting, neither should it be simply a haphazard affair that evolves in a spare room or the unused corner of a kitchen, bedroom, or den. There needs to be room for all types of equipment, not to mention surfaces for spreading projects out. And concerns such as seating, storage, lighting, and layouts must be taken into consideration when designing an appropriate home work space.

Basically, there are two ways to arrange work equipment in a home office: it can be concealed in closed cabinets and behind doors, or it can be placed out in the open and integrated into the decor of the room. Before deciding how to outfit your own space, consider which approach is most suitable, and keep in mind that the second arrangement demands discipline. Are you the kind of person who will really keep your desk clean and replace files when you're done working? If not, the first option may be more realistic, especially if your home office is situated in a space you share.

OPPOSITE: A campaign table tucked away in the corner of a room, backed by a credenza and two tall cabinets and flanked with a shelving unit, becomes an entire home office. Though crowded, the pieces are essentially clean-lined, which allows the space to work. ABOVE: A work space can be seamlessly introduced into any room with the right pieces. Here, a desk and chair are totally unobtrusive since they blend so well with the room's other furnishings.

Deciding what kind of work surface and storage system to use is another crucial component in planning a home office. Furniture firms, office supply stores, and catalogs offer thousands of alternatives, and if budget allows you can always hire a carpenter to tailor one to individual needs. In fact, there are so many options to choose from, and so many considerations to keep in mind (such as making sure critical pieces of equipment are easily accessible), that the prospect can be daunting.

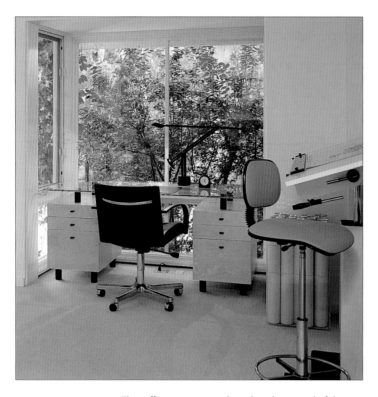

ABOVE: This office is arranged so that the wonderful view can provide inspiration for the person working at the desk. OPPOSITE: Form and function merge in this attic office set-up, where everything is accessible from behind a stunning but sensibly streamlined desk. Drawers, files, and even a drafting table are within "rolling" distance, the desktop is generous, and there's plenty of natural light and storage space.

Following are some pointers to keep in mind when planning a home office.

Layout

Before making any decisions on furnishings, take careful stock of the available space and the pieces you need to integrate into it. Unless all the elements of the office work together, the space will be ineffective. For instance, to avoid constantly getting up and down, keep storage for files near the area in which you plan to use them,

the printer close to the computer, and the phone within easy reach. If there are windows in the room, the desk should be situated nearby to take advantage of natural light, but keep in mind that when working on a computer, light, natural or artificial, behind the desk can cause glare on the monitor. Before filling the space, determine what you will need, what will fit, and where everything should go.

Furnishings

The pieces that are necessary for a home office can come in any and every incarnation, so it's possible to have the space match an existing decor; this is especially useful if the office is carved out of a fully furnished room. At the same time, for optimum efficiency, remember that pieces should be streamlined and simple rather than fussy and elaborate. The entire setup should be conceived for easy maintenance, and comfort, form, and function must merge in these furnishings.

Built-ins are one of the best ways to tailor a work space to specific or individual needs, and make it comfortable at the same time. They provide great storage space for virtually every item imaginable (books, equipment, files, even decorative objects). More important, they offer easy access to everything in them. And when ensconced behind closed cabinet-style shutters or

doors, they can endow a home office with a clean, uncluttered look, and give the users of the office a break: a mess may lurk behind the façade, and no one else will know. But built-ins stay put when you move, so consider setting up ready-made systems that can be disassembled if you don't own your home.

Other devices that can be employed to increase the flexibility of the space include modular pieces (for instance, two file cabinets topped with an attractive slab of Formica or wood can become a desk); pieces on wheels that can be rearranged easily as needs change; desktop organizers to keep clutter to a minimum (and cure a messy desk); and perhaps even comfort pieces if the space is large enough (such as a loveseat that folds out into a sleeper).

Lighting

Overhead lighting is only a start in a home office; it may be fine for everyday activities but anyone at work will need adequate task lighting. In addition, task lighting actually defines a work space, creating a subtle but undeniable boundary that sets it off from the rest of the room. Place versatile, flexible lamps (both their forms and wattage should be adjustable) everywhere you plan on working or reading.

OPPOSITE: Built-ins can help to tailor a workspace to individual needs, increase comfort, and mine every inch of storage space. Best of all, built-ins make it possible to keep everything at arm's length and increase the efficiency of the space. ABOVE: It doesn't take much effort to tailor furnishings to a specific space. Here, a simple plank desk and shelving system work perfectly and have an elegant appearance thanks to accessories such as a sleek chair and an Oriental carpet.

A B O V E : A small hobby corner has the potential of being a clutter hazard, but this well-organized station belonging to a dried-flower arranger seems to have clutter under control. O P P O S I T E : This built-in counter provides more than just a large work surface—it also has ample storage space for paint and other household necessities.

Lamps should be used wherever areas for work or reading are carved out in a room. And the more versatile and flexible they are, the more useful they will be in the long run. A desk lamp should have a bendable stem, swivel head, and two- or three-way illumination. A floor lamp should be adjustable to several heights and must be able to swivel, so that it can be directed to light a specific area.

Workrooms

A home art studio, sewing center, or machine shop all have lots of equipment to accommodate. Fitting these things into whatever space is available demands careful thought and planning.

Though the process for setting up a workroom is very similar to that of creating a home office, keep in mind that certain pursuits will need specialized and/or hardworking furnishings. If you're carving out a machine shop or sewing center, make sure work tables are roomy enough and can withstand the weight of the equipment; for an art studio, look for easy-clean surfaces. And tailor your storage to your activities, since all of these pursuits have radically different requisites. For instance, you may need deep drawers for textiles, wide flat drawers for artwork, or tiny drawers for screws and bits.

It's also important to decide how much equipment you want out in the open and how much to hide away behind cabinets. Part of that decision depends on where you have carved out

the work space and how neat it needs to look. If it's part of a high-traffic area, you won't want other family members tinkering with the tools of your trade or having to look at them constantly, so consider the closed-door approach. If you need to leave projects in progress spread out, consider locating the work table in an out-of-the-way corner of the room.

Finally, as in a home office, it's important to have adequate and appropriate lighting. An art studio will need natural light, while a sewing center or machine shop will need lots of task lighting. Keep this in mind when creating the work space.

Home Gyms

Unlike a home office or workroom, it's virtually impossible to hide away the equipment associated with a home gym. Despite the massive pieces of exercise equipment that this type of area calls for, it can still share space with other pursuits—consider using the large open expanses left over in any informal setting in the home. But since the equipment associated with this activity can be dangerous, station it in a spot where children won't be tempted to experiment with it. And for maximum effect, cluster the gym pieces close together in one part of the room—make sure that there's enough

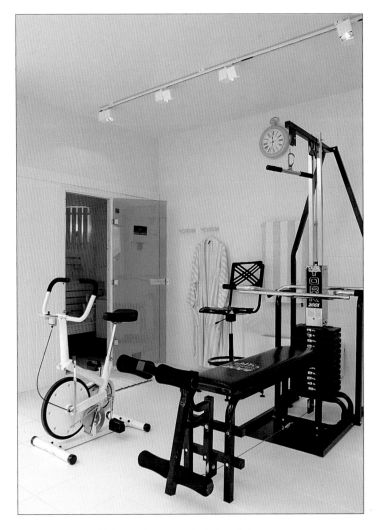

OPPOSITE: Built-in cabinets and shelves help organize a workspace and offer up lots of doors and drawers to screen items best left concealed. They also take on a much more elegant look when made in a luxurious dark wood and complemented by an attractive carpet. ABOVE: Gym equipment is impossible to hide, but doesn't have to be thrown haphazardly into a room. Here, a home gym displays a cohesive—and stylish—arrangement thanks to two tactics: clustering the equipment in one specific area and introducing a sporty black and yellow color scheme to create a sense of decor.

space to exercise comfortably. This leaves more space for other pursuits, and makes the gym space look more organized.

STORAGE SPACES

Everybody has something to store, from the avowed minimalist to the inveterate collector. It's virtually impossible to go through life without accruing at least the basics—a small wardrobe, some personal possessions, and a few accouterments for our homes.

But most of us acquire far more than just the basics—loads of clothes and scads of accessories, or furniture that is usually filled to the brim with ordinary caches of books, records, tapes, and compact disks, or with remarkable accumulations of objects and collectibles we just can't resist.

Then there are the necessities, almost never bare. We all need the prosaic elements of everyday life—towels, linens, toiletries, tools, kitchen utensils, cleaning supplies, or perhaps gardening equipment. And lest we forget in this age of physical fitness and electronic commuting, there are extras to contend with, too, sporting goods of every ilk, and home offices complete with a whole range of equipment and supplies.

Thus storage is a never-ending story, with an infinite array of plots. No one can afford to ignore it, since all of us have things to stash away. Without the order that proper storage imposes on our effects, chaos can reign supreme, so it's important to keep clutter from overwhelming our environments by employing some form of storage. The types to employ are as many and varied as the items there are to store, and they depend on individual needs. Some considerations to keep in mind are the nature of the residence, the make-up of the family unit, their lifestyles, and personal preferences.

Storage Considerations

Different kinds of residences allow for, and incorporate, different kinds of storage. Apartments lack the roomy expanses afforded by homes that have basements and attics, but many newer condominiums or lofts are built with loads of empty space just for this purpose. Older homes often have smaller closets and bathrooms, but frequently make up for this deficit with larger rooms that offer lots of possibilities for storage. Many also possess idiosyncratic nooks and crannies, such as large foyers or stairway landings, which can be utilized in alternative ways.

PAGE 108: Storage doesn't have to be boring. Drawers on casters conceal the utilitarian stuff but keep it within easy reach, while attractive glass cabinets show off interesting tableware. PAGE 109: An unusual chest with multisized drawers is not only an interesting focal point in a room, it offers up lots of storage for items in a variety of sizes. OPPOSITE: A bank of windows can provide challenges when storage and display are priorities. Here the problem is solved creatively with a shelf that does both. With its obvious Arts and Crafts detailing, it also strengthens the style quotient of the space and lends it architectural significance.

ABOVE: Some favor storage that incorporates display, while others favor hiding everything behind closed doors. This wall unit does a bit of both.

Family size is an obvious factor in determining storage needs. Children always take more space than expected, especially when they're small and have tiny togs but bulky gear, such as strollers, swings, play yards, or activity toys. Older children may need space for hoards of their own. Plus the more souls in a household, the more provisions, clothing, linens, and towels to stock in kitchens, closets, cabinets, and bathrooms.

Lifestyles—how people spend their time—may seem unrelated to storage, but they actually have a major impact on how space in a home is used. Avocations such as athletics, gardening, woodworking, reading, painting, sewing, knitting, or surfing the net all have equipment needs. And if the gear or supplies these pastimes call for aren't organized or within reach, it can be difficult to enjoy the activities.

Personal preference affects every aspect of storage. Some favor storage that incorporates display, while others hide everything away. But the issue is not quite this clear-cut. The potential display value of everyday objects is often overlooked, yet this is an often elegant and efficient approach to designing storage. Not only does it offer easy access to frequently used items, but if properly executed, it can make a space or accumulations of objects look remarkable. On the other hand, it can also be overdone, with too much left in the open, looking cluttered and collecting dust.

Concealed storage also has its strengths and weaknesses. It can be handsome and sleek, with everything in its own spot. But this often necessitates costly built-ins, and putting everything back right where it belongs requires discipline.

There's always the option of a happy medium, where prized or interesting possessions are put on show and mundane items are stowed away. But even achieving this balance isn't easy. So how can you plan adequate and appropriate storage for your residence, family unit, lifestyle, and preferences? Obvious as it may sound, start with the basics. Organizing a home doesn't always call for major upheavals or exorbitant expense. But it does call for forethought, planning, and prudence. And a little creativity, coupled with a lot of discipline, can also help matters.

Assessing Storage Needs

Experts say the first step is to take stock of everything you own. Go through every area of your home, and categorize, analyze, and purge. Much of what you own can probably be pared down, especially since there is no reason to save what you don't like, need, or use. These items only take up space and promote clutter.

Next, assess what's left, and separate everything into categories based on how frequently it all is used. Items on demand every day need to be readily accessible, while things used on a seasonal basis or sporadically can be put away. It makes good sense to rotate these things in and out of storage twice a year, since it helps keeps you

ABOVE: Open shelves can still achieve a "closed" or uniform appearance with the right tactics. Here, simple wicker baskets conceal odds and ends and present a united front.

organized by forcing you to view and reevaluate them. But keep a list of what gets stowed away in out-of-the-way storage, to make retrieval easier and to help you remember what you have.

After this process, you should be left with what really counts, and it's up to you to make the best of it. Begin the next step by taking complete stock of how you use your rooms. This will give you an idea of all the space at your disposal.

Reallocating these spaces sometimes makes sense, especially when storage issues are

ABOVE: Although this room is both a library and a dining area, the use of honey-colored wood throughout harmonizes the disparate elements. OPPOSITE: Every bit of available space was mined for storage in this carefully planned kitchen, right down to the space above its center island. A bank of shelves turns what would normally be dead space into an efficient and custom-fitted cabinet for dishes and wine.

concerned. A formal dining room, for example, can be combined with, or turned into, a library for someone with a massive book collection. Or a master suite can be used to consolidate bedrooms and a play area for a few children, freeing up several smaller rooms to be assigned new uses.

Many homes also have spaces that aren't part of specific rooms but offer up lots of square footage to adapt to storage, such as expansive

foyers, areas under the stairs, extra-large landings, or spacious circulation corridors. These are prime spots to put to good use. Just be careful that you don't impinge on the important traffic patterns in your home.

Once macro-space planning is done, it's time to fine-tune each room. A crowded eat-in kitchen may be given a "space" lift by carving out a pantry area, a dining room can hide a home office, or a master suite can house a whole gym. Flexibility and adaptability are the keys to success in this process.

Finally, micro-planning is the last step to making the most of storage in a home. The areas in each room that house clusters of stuff—such as cabinets, closets, and shelves—must be planned, organized, arranged, and constantly and consistently pruned. After all, everyone always needs more storage space than they actually have, so it's important to keep belongings in check. Following are some suggestions for planning storage for specific areas.

Kitchens

Like the hearth of yesteryear, the kitchen of today is the heart of a home. Every family member uses it at some time during the day, and the functions performed in this space are many and varied.

ABOVE: The work areas of a kitchen, which usually include the sink, refrigerator, and stove and/or cooktop, should be defined first, then storage should be arranged in clusters around them to heighten function and efficiency. OPPOSITE: While most kitchen storage is usually floor-to-ceiling built-in cabinetry split in the center with continuous countertops, the materials vary widely and can often be unusual or extraordinary.

Activities can revolve around its ascribed calling, namely preparing and partaking of nourishment, or may encompass all sorts of pastimes. Depending on its size and scope, parts of the kitchen are now used as a home office, craft area, playroom, and social center throughout the day. Thus it may be the busiest room in a residence, and as such must also be the home's most carefully planned, executed, and organized space.

Storage is the key to the success of this room; this is what keeps everything in order and out of the way. But space planning actually comes first. Before the requisite cabinets, shelves, or cupboards can be integrated into this room, the work areas of the space must be defined. Once the relationship of sink, cooking apparatus, and refrigerator is configured, it's possible to locate storage in logical clusters around them.

Most kitchen storage is floor-to-ceiling built-in cabinetry split in the center to accommodate continuous countertops used as work surfaces. The beauty of this system is that these cabinets hold all and hide all as needed. When fronted with see-through doors, they can also show all in a decorative fashion. Plus they can be customized with a wide range of interior fittings, such as drawers, dividers, shelves, racks, and carousels, or their design can incorporate such special features as pull-out components and chopping blocks.

Unfitted kitchens, composed of various types of freestanding storage, are another option, and allow great flexibility for those who like to rearrange their surroundings or move frequently. They also offer a wider decorative choice, since these pieces can range from antique to contemporary. In fact, the entire kitchen can become a much more eclectic and efficient environment with this approach. A large antique Welsh dresser, for instance, can be laden with accouterments, leaving the rest of the kitchen relatively free from clutter.

ABOVE: Appearances can be deceiving. A cabinet full of toys can lurk in a corner of the kitchen out of sight, keeping the space sleek and clutter-free. Most importantly, the toys are close at hand when they are needed. OPPOSITE: A collection of glass becomes an artistic display in this living room. When not in use, the TV set is cleverly hidden behind a painting that slides over the area.

Regardless of which type of kitchen you opt for, there are many other ways to coax storage spaces out of this room. First and foremost is to make sure that whatever type of cabinets are used in the room, they are mined to their maximum potential. Then study the room vertically and horizontally. Backs of doors can be fitted with shelves, racks, or grids; overhead racks suspended from ceilings can hold pots, pans, and

utensils; the bottoms of hanging cabinets can be fitted with hooks or holders for wine glasses, spice racks, or utensils; walls can be hung with grids or hooks to accommodate all sorts of items. Remember that all of these techniques demand heavy-duty anchoring so that the considerable weight of the kitchen equipment will not pull them out of walls. And they also require heavy-duty vigilance, since they will only be effective if they are used at all times.

Living and Dining Areas

Unlike other rooms in our homes such as the kitchen or bedroom, the living room doesn't have the clear-cut function it once possessed. Coupled with the demise of the formal dining room and the rise in combination spaces that incorporate both areas, this part of our homes is open to new interpretations. Living rooms are used in more ways than ever before, which greatly influences the way they are furnished and the kind of storage now included in their bounds.

Living rooms are rarely the stiff showpieces they once were; few of us have that kind of space to waste, and instead we truly live in this room these days. Such rooms often incorporate audio-visual equipment—which alone means a huge

ABOVE: A whole wall of built-in storage is not only far more effective and accommodating (in sheer cubic footage) than a breakfront or bureau in a dining room, it's also far more elementary since it lends a room cleaner lines.
OPPOSITE: Freestanding armoires can be integrated into any layout, and offer a particularly effective way to combine storage and display. Here, a set of white towels looks particularly attractive as it contrasts with the dark wood of the piece.

stock of things that need to be stored—and reading materials. Plus there are the objects we want to have on show, such as prized possessions, artworks, and collectibles, necessitating another kind of storage in the form of display. Storage is the key to a clutter-free, pristine environment.

Dining rooms have also changed; they are now rarely exclusive spaces devoted solely to one pursuit. As with living rooms, they can be combined with libraries, entertainment areas, home offices, family rooms, and even kitchens—quite a feat if a semblance of formal decorum is important to the homeowner. So along with the china, silver, linens, serving pieces, and other usual trappings a dining room must hold, there are all sorts of additional items to incorporate as well. Once again, adequate and efficient storage keeps clutter from overwhelming this space.

Creating good-looking storage for all these items can be challenging. It can be provided by built-ins or freestanding units, or an eclectic combination of both, which can add character and variety to a space. While all storage units are similar in substance, since they all hold things, they can be quite different in style. Thus built-ins can be fashioned in any decorative style—Colonial, Arts and Crafts, or high-tech, for example—and freestanding units can take shapes that range from vintage armoires to sleek postmodern pieces.

Manipulating storage is another issue that must be addressed in these areas, since both built-ins and freestanding pieces can fade into the background or can be used to define a room. Natural recesses, such as alcoves or the spaces surrounding mantels, or whole blank walls are ideal and unobtrusive spots for either built-in or freestanding storage, especially if the freestanding piece fits the niche exactly and mimics a built-in. But large shelving systems, or even shorter units placed back-to-back, can also become room dividers, fronting on both spaces.

Bed and Bath

Space always seems to be at a premium, which may explain why bedrooms and bathrooms are gradually becoming more multipurpose spaces. While they are still devoted to beds, clothes, and toiletries, they can also incorporate furnishings, equipment, and accessories devoted to many other pursuits. There may be shelves filled with books, a cushy chair for reading, the fixings for a home office, or gym gear. In fact, we cram so many functions into bedrooms, closets, and washrooms these days—from sleeping, reading, and watching

built-in pieces can be integrated into all these potential layouts; the area under the bed can become another source of storage.

Closets are also up for grabs these days—anything goes as long as it makes the most of a space. Many closets are supplied with expensive built-ins with special fittings that mine every square inch of space, while others are sensibly arranged with economical wire systems—combining hanging fixtures and stacking baskets—that are just as effective and easier to adapt to changing needs. And extra-large closets can double as dressing rooms if they have a central area in which users can move around.

Perhaps the greatest strides have been made where bathrooms are concerned, since many seem to have more square footage than ever before. Many of these bigger spaces incorporate large sink areas or expansive vanities with ample storage underneath, or have whole walls devoted to built-in storage. But integrating storage into smaller bathrooms still takes ingenuity and planning. It's possible to "pull" space from almost anywhere, by adding alcoves to the ends or sides of tubs for towel storage, placing small chests under basins, adding shelving over toilets, or adding corner shelves. In fact, space is there for the taking in all of these rooms; it just requires a little creativity and a lot of sensible design.

television to working out, washing, and dressing—that their organizational perfection is imperative.

The one thing all bedrooms obviously have in common is the bed, which can and often does dominate the space. The way this piece is situated in the room dictates storage scenarios. Placing a bed in the middle of a wall can create alcoves, while moving it toward one corner leaves room for larger storage units. Placing it in the middle of a space grants lots of creative leeway: the area between the bed and wall can become a dressing room, private study, or home office bounded by a shelving system, while its back can become a headboard for the bed. Both freestanding and

OPPOSITE: Glass shelves can be integrated into almost any layout, and offer a particularly effective way to combine storage and display. ABOVE: Space is there for the taking in any room, even a tiny bathroom. A cabinet and ledge don't have to flank or surround the sink; here they're assigned to an empty corner, giving the tiny room a spacious feeling.

Special Spaces

Planning storage systems for specific rooms is an obvious endeavor; recognizing that there are many other parts of a home to organize or adapt in the same way is the final step to addressing storage concerns. Always try to make the most of every existing area—attics and basements, storage lockers in apartments or condominiums, extra-large hallways and landings, spaces under stairs or eaves, mud or utility rooms, or oversized garages or storage sheds.

Attics and basements can add significant living and storage space to a home, and often the uses made of these areas combine both functions. A home office or playroom in an attic, or a craft corner and hobby center in a basement, all require room for activities and storage. Often the storage component of the space can be used to define activity centers. Shelves can become a freestanding wall that separates areas such as the office and playroom that coexist in the same attic. Both attic and basement also offer ideal spots for seasonal storage, and again, thoughtful design can allow these spaces to combine this function with other uses.

Extra-large hallways and landings and the triangular spaces under stairs or eaves are all found spaces. They're often roomy enough to double as

OPPOSITE, TOP: Unique storage alternatives can often work surprisingly well in unique spaces, as shown by this curved staircase paired with a curved bureau. OPPOSITE, BOTTOM: This laundry room incorporates plenty of storage, an oversized countertop that comes in handy for folding, and excellent lighting. And when the machines aren't being used, they are tucked away behind wooden cabinet doors. ABOVE: Free up floor space in living areas by mining the triangular space under a stairway. With proper planning, design, and execution, a built-in unit can offer up extensive and attractive storage space.

storage areas, freeing up floor space in living areas. An entire library can be lodged on one side of a wide staircase (which is just one variety of hallway), or line a sizable second-floor landing. Or a whole home office or spacious closet can be worked into the oddly shaped alcoves under stairs. Because these areas are actually alcoves and recesses, they can accommodate built-in or set-in storage systems fairly unobtrusively.

Mud or utility rooms and oversized garages or storage sheds are often-neglected spaces begging for attention. Instead of letting them become cluttered zones or oversized junk drawers, take advantage of their potential. Mud and utility rooms are naturals as an extra source of convenient storage. And garages or sheds can become perfect areas for seasonal storage or craft centers, especially if a home is short on space. Like other areas in a home, they can be outfitted with attractive and carefully planned built-in or freestanding storage. The most sensible options in these spaces are cost-effective systems.

Sources

Page 2
Richard Eustace, designer
Boston, MA
(617) 367-8116

Pages 21, 64, 75, 80
architects:
Chuck Dietsche
Wilmington, NC
(910) 251-8340
Dan Costa
Boston, MA
(617) 451-5898

Pages 34, 54, 78 bottom
Madeline Stuart, designer
Los Angeles, CA
(213) 935-3305

Page 41
John Silverio, architect
Lincolnville, ME
(207) 763-3885

Pages 44, 70
Christopher Coleman, designer
New York, NY
(212) 616-8663

Page 49
Benn Theodore Inc., designer
Boston, MA
(617) 227-1915

Page 64
Kalman Construction, builders
Nantucket, MA
508-228-5825

Pages 65, 82
Robin Piccone, designer
Los Angeles, CA
(213) 464-8350

Page 86
Kathy St. Claire of Ken Topping Home
Improvements
San Francisco, CA
(415) 731-3930

Page 88
Michele Foster, Foster Associates, designer
Portsmouth, RI
(401) 682-1633

Pages 90, 102
Miller/Stein Interior Design
Menlo Park, CA
(650) 328-1610

Page 93
Karyne Johnson, Panache Interiors
Darien, CT
(203) 655-5143

Page 94
Peter Wheeler, PJ Wheeler Associates,
designer
Boston, MA
(617) 426-5921

Page 97
Mark Landsberg & Associates, architects
Newtonville, MA
(617) 969-1191

Page 98
Agnes Bourne, Inc., designer
San Francisco, CA
(415) 626-6883

Page 106
Stone-Wood, designer
Sacramento, CA
(916) 454-1506

Page 111
Charles Bohl, architect
Annapolis, MD
(410) 269-8028

Page 118
Sharon Campbell Interior Design
San Anselmo, CA
(415) 453-2323

Page 122
Wright Design
Corte Madera, CA
(415) 924-2203

Index

Photo Credits

©Antoine Bootz: 9, 14, 22 top, 42, 57, 58, 72 both; 10, 13, 48 top, 68 top, 79, 81 bottom, 88 top (designer: Alexander Julian); 15, 62 (designer: Mary Cooper); 55, 66, 71 (architect: Dennis Wedlick); 63, 77, 99 (designers: Bentley, La Rosa, Salasky); 101 (designer: Michael Toth Design)

Courtesy of California Closets: 84 both

©Grey Crawford: 23, 100, 119, 120

©Elizabeth Whiting Associates: 3, 5, 16, 17, 19, 20, 24, 27 bottom, 29 bottom, 30 top, 31, 32, 39, 59, 60, 61, 68 bottom, 73, 74, 81 top, 85 bottom, 107, 108, 113, 124 bottom, 125 both

©Michael Garland: 26 top (designer: Joe Ruggiero), 104, 116 (designer: Chris Barrett Design)

©Tria Giovan: 51

©Steve Gross & Susan Daley: 21 (architects: Chuck Dietsche and Dan Costa), 30 bottom (designers: Jerry Lombardi and Michael Fiur), 37, 40 bottom (designer: Melissa Price), 53, 56 (designer: Jane Kilpatrick-Schott), 64 top (architects: Chuck Dietsche and Dan Costa), 75 top (architects: Chuck Dietsche and Dan Costa), 80 (architects: Chuck Dietsche and Dan Costa), 85 top, 111 (architect: Charles Bohl), 115

©Nancy Hill: 93 (designer: Karyne Johnson), 95 (CMC Designs), 96 bottom

The Interior Archive: 33; ©Schulenburg: 25, 117

©David Livingston: 83, 90 (designer: Miller/Stein Interior Design), 98 (designer: Agnes Bourne), 102 (designer: Miller/Stein Interior Design), 103, 106 (designer: Stone Wood), 112, 114, 118 (designer: Sharon Campbell Interior Design), 122 (designer: Wright Design)

©Kit Morris: 86 (designer: Kathy St. Claire of Ken Topping Home Improvements)

©Robert Perron: 26 bottom (designer: Charles Spada)

©Paul Rocheleau: 22 bottom, 28, 91

©Eric Roth: 2 (designer: Richard Eustice), 35 (designer: Paul Magnuson), 49 (designer: Benn Theodore), 64 bottom (construction: Kalman Construction), 67, 69, 75 bottom, 76, 87, 88 bottom, (designer: Michael Foster of Foster Associates 94 (designer: Peter Wheeler of PJ Wheeler Associates), 97 (designer: Mark Landsberg & Associates), 109, 124 top (designer: Françoise Theise of Adesso)

©Keith Scott Morton: 105

©Franca Speranza: 89

©Tim Street-Porter: 29 top (designer: Kathleen Speiglewan), 38 (designer: Smith-Miller), 40 top (designer: Larry Totah)

©Brian Vanden Brink: 27 top, 41 (architect: John Silverio)

©Dominique Vorillon: 6 (designer: Angelil/Graham), 34 (designer: Madeline Stuart), 36 (designer: Angelil/Stuart), 43 (designer: Russell Simpson), 44 (designer: Christopher Coleman), 45, 46, 47, 48 bottom (designer: Patrick Dune), 52, 54 (designer: Madeline Stuart), 65 (designer: Robin Piccone), 70 (designer: Christopher Coleman), 78 top (designer: Patrick Dune), 78 bottom (designer: Madeline Stuart), 82 (designer: Robin Piccone), 96 top, 121 (designer: Patrick Dune), 123 (designer: L. O'Herlihy)